D1356898

THE BEST OF
BRITISH COMEDY

DAD'S
ARMY

THE BEST OF
BRITISH COMEDY

DAD'S ARMY

THE BEST SCENES, JOKES AND ONE-LINERS

Richard Webber

HarperCollins*Publishers*

HarperCollins*Publishers*
77–85 Fulham Palace Road,
Hammersmith, London W6 8JB

First published by HarperCollins*Publishers* 2008

2

Scripts © Jimmy Perry and David Croft
© Richard Webber Ltd 2008

The Author asserts the moral right to
be identified as the author of this work

A catalogue record for this book
is available from the British Library

ISBN-10 0-00-728530-2
ISBN-13 978-0-00-728530-3

Printed and bound in the UK by
Butler Tanner and Dennis

Picture credits: © BBC Photo Library pp. 61, 85, 91,
115, 147; © Radio Times pp. 14, 39, 45, 64, 67, 76,
79, 95, 97, 112, 128, 133, 145; © Mirrorpix pp. 2, 10,
12, 15, 26, 47, 104, 109.

ACKNOWLEDGEMENTS

I would like to thank Jimmy Perry and David Croft for, once again, allowing me to use script extracts and giving up more time to be interviewed about *Dad's Army*. Thanks, also, to the actors I spoke to in the course of compiling this book, including Bill Pertwee, Ian Lavender, Clive Dunn, Pamela Cundell, Philip Madoc, Eric Longworth and Frank Williams. And I'm grateful to John Laurie's daughter, Veronica, and Edward Sinclair's son, Peter. Last, but by no means least, thank you to my agent, Jeffrey Simmons, Don Smith and my editor, Natalie Jerome, at HarperCollins.

EPISODE LIST

Series One

1. 'The Man And The Hour' (Transmitted 31/7/68)
2. 'Museum Piece' (7/8/68)
3. 'Command Decision' (14/8/68)
4. 'The Enemy Within The Gates' (28/8/68)
5. 'The Showing Up Of Corporal Jones' (4/9/68)
6. 'Shooting Pains' (11/9/68)

Series Two

1. 'Operation Kilt' (1/3/69)
2. 'The Battle Of Godfrey's Cottage' (8/3/69)
3. 'The Loneliness Of The Long-distance Walker'
   (15/3/69)
4. 'Sergeant Wilson's Little Secret' (22/3/69)
5. 'A Stripe For Frazer' (29/3/69)
6. 'Under Fire' (5/4/69)

Series Three

Series Four

6. 'Absent Friends' (30/10/70)
7. 'Put That Light Out!' (6/11/70)
8. 'The Two And A Half Feathers' (13/11/70)
9. 'Mum's Army' (20/11/70)
10. 'The Test' (27/11/70)
11. 'A Wilson (Manager)?' (4/12/70)
12. 'Uninvited Guests' (11/12/70)
13. 'Fallen Idol' (18/12/70)

Christmas Special

'Battle Of The Giants' (27/12/71)

Series Five

1. 'Asleep In The Deep' (6/10/72)
2. 'Keep Young And Beautiful' (13/10/72)
3. 'A Soldier's Farewell' (20/10/72)
4. 'Getting The Bird' (27/10/72)
5. 'The Desperate Drive Of Corporal Jones' (3/11/72)
6. 'If The Cap Fits …' (10/11/72)
7. 'The King Was In His Counting House' (17/11/72)
8. 'All Is Safely Gathered In' (24/11/72)
9. 'When Did You Last See Your Money?' (1/12/72)
10. 'Brain Versus Brawn' (8/12/72)

11. 'A Brush With The Law' (15/12/72)
12. 'Round and Round Went The Great Big Wheel' (22/12/72)
13. 'Time On My Hands' (29/12/72)

Series Six

1. 'The Deadly Attachment' (31/10/73)
2. 'My British Buddy' (7/11/73)
3. 'The Royal Train' (14/11/73)
4. 'We Know Our Onions' (21/11/73)
5. 'The Honourable Man' (28/11/73)
6. 'Things That Go Bump In The Night' (5/12/73)
7. 'The Recruit' (12/12/73)

Series Seven

1. 'Everybody's Trucking' (15/11/74)
2. 'A Man Of Action' (22/11/74)
3. 'Gorilla Warfare' (29/11/74)
4. 'The Godiva Affair' (6/12/74)
5. 'The Captain's Car' (13/12/74)
6. 'Turkey Dinner' (23/12/74)

Series Eight

1. 'Ring Dem Bells' (5/9/75)
2. 'When You've Got To Go' (12/9/75)
3. 'Is There Honey Still For Tea?' (19/9/75)
4. 'Come In, Your Time Is Up' (26/9/75)
5. 'High Finance' (3/10/75)
6. 'The Face On The Poster' (10/10/75)

Christmas Special

'My Brother And I' (26/12/75)

Christmas Special

'The Love Of Three Oranges' (26/12/75)

Series Nine

1. 'Wake-Up Walmington' (2/10/77)
2. 'The Making Of Private Pike' (9/10/77)
3. 'Knights Of Madness' (16/10/77)
4. 'The Miser's Hoard' (23/10/77)
5. 'Number Engaged' (6/11/77)
6. 'Never Too Old' (13/11/77)

INTRODUCTION

In the annals of British television, no finer example of classic comedy exists than in the shape of *Dad's Army*, the Home Guard-based sitcom written by veteran writers Jimmy Perry and David Croft. Although they penned many other sterling programmes, including *Hi-De-Hi!* and the underrated *You Rang, M'Lord?*, they'll forever be remembered for their brilliant wartime comedy spotlighting the antics of the Walmington-on-Sea Home Guard, led by the irascible and pompous Captain Mainwaring.

Between 1968 and 1977, nine series and three Christmas Specials – totalling 80 instalments – were screened, much to the delight of the millions of fans who tuned in; but the show's popularity has continued unabated and even today, four decades since the platoon marched onto the scene, it remains one of the golden offerings from the sitcom genre.

Unlike most situation comedies which highlight one or two key characters, *Dad's Army* was team comedy of the highest order. Although much of the focus concentrated on the relationships between Mainwaring and Wilson (adroitly played by Arthur Lowe and John Le Mesurier respectively) within Swallow Bank during the day and the coastal town's Home Guard by night, the disparate bunch of individuals making up the bravehearted platoon was equally valuable to the overall success of the show. Who can forget Corporal 'Don't Panic!' Jones; the mollycoddled Private Pike; Frazer, the doom-and-gloom merchant; Walker, the

He may have driven Mainwaring mad at times but there was no doubting Jones' bravery.

kindhearted spiv and doddery old Private Godfrey, who was forever nipping off to spend a penny, much to Mainwaring's chagrin. And let's not forget the sniping Mr Yeatman, the huffy Vicar and, of course, loud-mouthed Warden Hodges.

Within this celebration of *Dad's Army*, I've selected some of the best scenes from the series. Of course, the selection process is subjective and I could have included hundreds more

'I'm afraid I must have dozed off for a minute.' (Godfrey)

snatches of dialogue to highlight just how good the series was. Much of the humour in Croft and Perry's sitcom emanates from the actors' performances, how they bring the scripts alive and the interaction in front of the cameras; but the following scenes – which were taken directly from the scripts and, therefore, may differ slightly from the screened version – are fitting examples from arguably Britain's best sitcom – well, in my eyes anyway.

As well as script extracts, this book contains lots of goodies for *Dad's Army* fans, including the story behind the programme's success, a collection of fascinating facts regarding the show, memories from those who worked on the project and much, much more. Happy reading!

RICHARD WEBBER

THE STORY IN
A NUTSHELL

While travelling by train to the East London suburb of Stratford East, actor-turned-scriptwriter Jimmy Perry dreamt up an idea that would not only alter the course of his career but provide the rest of us with something rather special.

At the time, Perry was treading the boards at Stratford East's Theatre Royal, working for stage director Joan Littlewood; but for some time he'd harboured dreams of writing for television, despite having only written for pantomimes and comedy sketches. Although he'd never penned material for the small screen, he was driven by the desire to write something in order to create a significant part for himself.

On his daily commutes across London, he began formulating a premise. Realising it would be judicious to write about something he'd experienced and understood, and backed by the knowledge that service-based comedies like *Bilko* and *The Army Game* had been successful, he turned his attention to the Home Guard.

Using the Home Guard as the foundations for a sitcom hadn't been tackled before. But having served with units in Barnes and Watford as a teenager, it seemed the best course of action. This was 1967, however, more than two decades since the Second World War had finished, and Perry's enthusiasm was initially dampened by doubts regarding whether anyone would remember the Home Guard's contribution during the war; his mood wasn't helped when he visited the local library. When he asked the librarian for books about the Home Guard, his request was met with a quizzical stare.

Unperturbed, Perry began work on a synopsis and a draft script, inspired by the Will Hay film, *Oh! Mr Porter*. The balance of characters, comprising a pompous man, a boy and an old man was, in Perry's eyes, the perfect combination. Influenced by this screen classic, Perry wrote a script, titled *The Fighting Tigers*, but didn't actively market the work for many weeks,

'Don't panic!' (Jones)

concentrating, instead, on his work with Joan Littlewood. It wasn't until 1967, during a summer break with the theatre, that Perry proactively tried selling his Home Guard effort. While appearing in an episode of the TV series, *Beggar My Neighbour*, Perry grasped the opportunity of approaching the director of the sitcom, David Croft, and telling him about his idea for a Home Guard-based sitcom. Croft agreed to read it and was suitably impressed. When a second script had been written, Croft discussed the would-be project with Michael Mills, the BBC's then Head of Light Entertainment, who was prepared to green light the project so long as David Croft – who was an experienced TV writer – co-wrote the sitcom; it was also Mills who, disliking Perry's proposed title, dreamt up the name, *Dad's Army*.

Although a few concerns were expressed within the BBC regarding whether the project was taking the mickey out of the Home Guard, most people supported the idea as Perry and

Did you know?

Writers Jimmy Perry and David Croft considered calling time on the sitcom in 1975 until David Attenborough, the then Controller of BBC1, persuaded them to continue. The show ran for another two Christmas Specials and a complete series.

Croft's attention turned to refining the characters, among them a spiv, a common wartime character, and an ageing war veteran, based on a man who served with Jimmy Perry in the Home Guard and fought at the Battle of Omdurman in 1898.

The character of Godfrey, meanwhile, stemmed from the writers' wish to create a gentle character, while the mollycoddled Pike was based on Perry's experiences as a boy and Hodges introduced to upset the pompous Captain Mainwaring, thereby generating many situations from which comedy could be mined.

When it was time for casting, Jimmy Perry hoped to play Walker, the spiv, a role he'd created for himself; sadly, for him, director and co-writer David Croft had other ideas. Wanting Perry behind the camera, Jimmy Beck was recruited, although Perry suggested Arthur English. While Michael Mills acquired the services of John Le Mesurier and John Laurie, Perry claims the credit for securing Arthur Lowe as Mainwaring, even though it was a struggle convincing some quarters. Lowe had made his name on the small screen playing Mr Swindley in *Coronation Street*: but that was commercial TV. Unsure about his suitability, film actor Thorley Walters and Jon Pertwee, whose later credits included *Doctor Who*, were offered the part before Arthur Lowe was invited to the BBC to discuss the role and subsequently offered the job, quickly making it his own.

Arnold Ridley had worked for Croft on *Hugh and I* while Jones, the butcher, was originally offered to Jack Haig. But when he accepted a 26-episode children's series, *Wacky Jacky*, instead, Clive Dunn was offered the role which, after some deliberation, he accepted. With Ian Lavender enrolled to play young Frank Pike, Bill Pertwee as Hodges, Frank Williams as the Vicar and the underrated Edward Sinclair as the Verger, the main cast was in place and the cameras were ready to roll.

Location filming took place in and around Thetford, Norfolk, using the open spaces of the military training grounds. After the interior scenes were recorded at BBC Television Centre, the first episode, 'The Man And The Hour', was transmitted on 31st July 1968 and met with a mixed reaction from the press. Meanwhile, the results from an audience survey requested by David Croft were so negative he prevented the results reaching his bosses, fearing they would pull the plug on the show. Thankfully, the sitcom was given the chance to mature and before long its popularity was growing.

The show ran for nine series, plus Christmas Specials, over a period of nine years but there was a moment, in 1975, when its future was uncertain. Perry and Croft were enjoying success with the *Dad's Army* stage show, which afforded them the opportunity to assess whether they wanted to continue with the TV series. Fortunately for the show's many fans, the then controller of BBC1, David Attenborough, wined and dined Perry and Croft and persuaded them to continue.

The last series ran through Autumn 1977, culminating in 'Never Too Old', an episode which saw Corporal Jones and Mrs Fox finally tie the knot. It was the end of an era but little did anyone know that the programme would carry on entertaining millions for decades to come.

'THE MAN AND THE HOUR'

Mainwaring begins interviewing the Walmington residents who've volunteered to join the Home Guard. Wilson, who's been made sergeant, doesn't bark out the commands as Mainwaring would like.

Wilson asks the first volunteer to enter the office.

WILSON: Would you mind stepping this way, please?

MAINWARING: Sergeant Wilson, come here. I intend to mould those men out there into an aggressive fighting unit. I'm going to lead them, command them, and inspire them to become ruthless killers, but I'm not going to get very far if you keep inviting them to 'step this way'. 'Quick march' is the order, Wilson.

WILSON: I'm sorry, sir. (*To the man who's already standing at the table*) Quick march!

FRAZER: There's not much point, I'm here already.

MAINWARING: Name, please?

FRAZER: James Frazer.

'Can I be excused?' (Godfrey)

MAINWARING: Occupation?

FRAZER: I keep a philatelist's shop.

MAINWARING: How d'you spell that?

FRAZER: S ... H ... O ... P ...

Bill Pertwee revelled in his role as loud-mouthed Hodges.

Memories ...

'I'll never forget the first day of filming because it snowed – and it was supposed to be summer! I don't think it showed, though. When it finally stopped and we were ready to do the first shot, David [Croft] asked me to go and get everyone. A lot of them were sitting in David's Rolls-Royce, so I opened the door, saying: "OK, chaps, we're ready to go now." I didn't know what they'd be like, I thought they'd be enthusiastic but Arthur replied: "We'll come when we're ready." I went back to David and said: "We've got a right lot of miserable sods here, David!" They were hard-nosed old pros but bloody good: they knew their job, that's the main thing.'

JIMMY PERRY

Arthur Lowe was third choice to play Captain Mainwaring.

Memories ...

'Arthur Lowe was a good all-round actor, very experienced, and was able to call upon all these little mannerisms. He could be obstructive and awkward but if you knew how to handle him, he was fine. He was an old actor and we understood him well and he understood us. The important thing was not to drive him into a corner or get fundamental opinions from him. I never asked the actors what they thought of things, it was safer that way. Arthur's character meant he could be pedantic and like Mainwaring at times, but then all the actors were like their characters, to a point.

'He wasn't prepared to welcome the public. Once, a member of the public had got autographs of all the other actors. He was talking to his friend, who asked whether he had Mainwaring's? He replied: "No, he's a miserable old toad." Arthur had waved him away. He said: "I don't do that when I'm working." Bill Pertwee actually told the story at dinner that night, and Joan, Arthur's wife, said: "There you are, Arthur, that's the image you project." He did, however, have the grace to laugh at himself.

'I'll always remember how much he loved his food and was often late getting on the coach in the mornings. It was no good taking him away until he'd *been*. He was a lovely man but the whole schedule was built around Arthur Lowe's bowels!'

DAVID CROFT

'THE LONELINESS OF THE LONG-DISTANCE WALKER'

Walker has just announced he's been called up. The members of the platoon, however, have other things on their minds.

It's not good news for the platoon when Walker receives his call-up.

FRAZER: This is terrible news, Joe, terrible! What about my whisky?

JONES: And my gin?

GODFREY: What about my sisters' fudge?

PIKE: What about my mum's elastic?

MAINWARING: Don't be selfish, men. We mustn't think about ourselves. By the way, what about *my* whisky?

Jimmy Beck trained as an artist before turning to acting.

Memories ...

'Jimmy Beck was my first choice to play Walker. Jimmy Perry wrote the part for himself but I didn't want that to happen because although he was a very good actor and would have been fine in the part, I didn't want an actor who'd written the show taking part. Firstly, everyone would think he'd written himself the best part and I wouldn't have had his influence at rehearsals and during the recordings.

'I'd worked with Jimmy Beck before, not in any big capacity, but his career was going great guns and he was obviously a very talented performer. He did a good job and gave a very funny interpretation.'

DAVID CROFT

'THE LION HAS PHONES'

Jones, inside a phone box, tries reporting an enemy plane has crashed. Unfortunately, he's incorrectly connected to the local cinema.

JONES: Major Brooks?

DOREEN: (*With puzzled look at receiver*) Yes, that's right.

JONES: Can you help me?

DOREEN: Certainly, sir … *One of Our Aircraft is Missing*.

JONES: That's funny, I thought it was one of theirs.

DOREEN: No … it's *One of Our Aircraft is Missing*. It went up five minutes ago.

JONES: Well, it's come down now.

DOREEN: No, sir ... it doesn't come down till 10.30 ... if you hurry you'll just catch it. Eric Portman and Googie Withers are in it.

'Stupid boy!' (Mainwaring)

JONES: Well, why are they shooting at us?

DOREEN: No, sir ... they're not still shooting it ... it's finished.

Did you know?

Some of the characters' names were altered before the first episode was made: while Private Frazer was originally to be called Private Duck and Joe Walker was Joe Fish, Jack Jones started life as Jim and was going to have a twin brother, George.

Memories ...

'I took a while to accept the part because I was worried about how they'd treat the sergeant. Alfie Bass and Bill Fraser were in *The Army Game* and Bill Fraser did a rather old-fashioned sergeant; I was concerned they might choose someone to play the sergeant like that. But it was brilliant casting when John Le Mesurier was asked to play the character. When he said he was going to do it, I agreed, too. I didn't know Arthur Lowe's work at all, or any of the other guys except John Le Mesurier, so when I knew he was going to be in it, I knew I had a mate there.'

CLIVE DUNN

'SOMETHING NASTY IN THE VAULT'

Mainwaring and Wilson are stuck in the bank's strong room. There has been an air raid and they've ended up holding an unexploded bomb. Pike arrives.

PIKE: Uncle Arthur?

WILSON: Oh, what it is, Frank?

PIKE: Do you think I ought to phone mum and tell her you're holding a bomb?

WILSON: No!

PIKE: But she might get cross if she found out that you'd been holding a bomb and she wasn't told about it.

Memories …

'In a way, Ian Lavender was playing a young person similar to me in the Home Guard. But what we really wanted was a soppy boy. When you have a lot of old men, it's funny to have a young person amongst them; it makes for a lot of humour.'

JIMMY PERRY

Memories ...

'I have fond memories of "The Day The Balloon Went Up" and remember marching across a field holding on to the barrage balloon with strict instructions not to wind the cord around our hands because if the balloon did escape, we'd have been pulled up with it. David [Croft] said: "If you can't hold the cord, why don't you put your hands together as if you're in prayer." It was a funny moment.'

FRANK WILLIAMS

'WAR DANCE'

Mainwaring is sporting a black eye so Godfrey and his sister suggest various remedies.

GODFREY: You remember my sister, Mr Mainwaring? By Jove, that eye looks nasty.

MAINWARING: I rather stupidly walked into the door of the linen cupboard.

CISSY: A little bit of folded Christmas card is awfully good for that.

MAINWARING: For a black eye?

CISSY: No, for keeping the linen cupboard door shut.

GODFREY: What you need, Mr Mainwaring, is a hot onion.

MAINWARING: On the eye?

CISSY: No, Charles, that's for earache.

GODFREY: No, dear, it's a mustard plaster for earache.

CISSY: No, Charles, that's for backache.

GODFREY: It's all rather muddling, isn't it?

'BRANDED'

Godfrey is planning to resign from the Home Guard and explains he made his decision whilst making the tea.

GODFREY: Oh yes – well, I went into the larder to get the milk, then I saw something that made me realise that I just couldn't carry on.

MAINWARING: What on earth was it?

GODFREY: A mouse.

MAINWARING: A mouse?

GODFREY: Yes, you see in the larder was a great big, empty pudding basin – a mouse had fallen inside and it was running round and round trying to get out. I know I ought to kill it because we're overrun with mice, so I got hold of it, and as I

held it in my hand I could feel its little heart beating under its fur – and I just couldn't bring myself to do it.

MAINWARING: So, what did you do?

GODFREY: I took it out in the garden and let it go.

MAINWARING: Look, Godfrey, I still don't see what this has got to do with you wanting to leave the platoon?

GODFREY: Don't you understand, sir? If I couldn't bring myself to kill that mouse, how could I ever kill a German?

....

After saving Mainwaring's life while on exercise, Godfrey – who's been sent to Coventry since admitting he's a conscientious objector – is recovering at home when the platoon pays a visit.

CISSY: My brother will see you now, Mr Mainwaring.

MAINWARING: Thank you, Miss Godfrey … Well, Godfrey … er, feeling better?

Arnold Ridley, who played Mr Godfrey, was the oldest member of the cast.

GODFREY: Yes. Thank you, sir.

PIKE: Some flowers, Mr Godfrey.

GODFREY: Thank you.

JONES: Some strengthening sweetbreads.

FRAZER: I've brought you a bottle of Scotch.

WALKER: I've brought you a quarter of tea.

GODFREY: From the Army and Navy?

WALKER: No, from a fellow I know in the Air Force.

WILSON: (*Whispering to Mainwaring*) Well, aren't you going to thank him for saving your life, sir?

MAINWARING: (*Hissing back*) Yes, of course I am. (*He clears his throat*) Now, look here, Godfrey – I may have said a few harsh things in the past – but I want you to know that I ... deep down (*He shuffles his feet and looks around the room – looks at a photograph above the bed*) What's this photograph of you in uniform, Godfrey?

Memories …

'Being a conscientious objector was a difficult thing to be. There was no sympathy for them, they were scrutinised very closely.'

DAVID CROFT

'I was in the war and don't have much time for conscientious objectors. This was a lovely episode and we included all the old sayings about, "What's a matter with you, don't you want to fight?" and "You're not normal." It worked very well, and the tag was that Godfrey had won a Military Medal.'

JIMMY PERRY

GODFREY: It was in the last war, sir.

MAINWARING: You're wearing the Military Medal.

GODFREY: Yes, I know.

MAINWARING: But you told me you were a damn conchie – I mean a conscientious objector.

> ### Did you know?
> Ian Lavender was only 22 when called up to play Pikey. But he was already turning grey, so dye and Brylcreem were used to disguise his natural colour.

GODFREY: So I was, sir.

MAINWARING: Then how did you win the Military Medal?

CISSY: He volunteered as a medical orderly. My brother wouldn't tell you himself, Mr Mainwaring, but during the Battle of the Somme, he went out into no-man's land under heavy fire and saved several lives.

GODFREY: It wasn't very …

The men all stare with open mouths.

JONES: Sorry, we've all stood upon you in false judgement, Mr Godfrey.

FRAZER: Speaking for myself, I never doubted you for a single minute.

WILSON: (*To Mainwaring*) Perhaps in future Godfrey could be our medical orderly, sir.

MAINWARING: Thank you, Wilson, that's an excellent idea. As from today, Godfrey, you're appointed platoon Medical Orderly – report back as soon as you're fit.

GODFREY: Thank you, sir.

MAINWARING: Well, we mustn't tire you anymore. Goodbye, Godfrey.

GODFREY: Goodbye, sir.

They all start to go.

MAINWARING: There's still one thing I can't understand, Godfrey.

GODFREY: What's that, sir?

MAINWARING: Why didn't you wear your medals?

GODFREY: Somehow I thought they looked rather ostentatious, sir.

MAINWARING: Ostentatious … but good Lord, man – if I'd have won the Military Medal, I'd have worn it proudly on my chest for the world to see.

'Right, now pay attention, all of you.' (Mainwaring)

GODFREY: Yes, sir, and that would have been all right – because somehow you look like a hero.

WILSON: It just goes to show, sir, you can never judge by appearances.

Mainwaring gives him a terrible glare.

'SONS OF THE SEA'

The platoon is lost in a boat whilst undertaking river patrols.
Everyone has their own ideas regarding finding north.

WILSON: If we could find the north, sir, and row towards it – that
would take us back to the shore.

MAINWARING: Excellent, Wilson – where's the north, Frazer?

FRAZER: Why ask me? You're the one who's supposed to know.
Have another look at the back of your hand.

MAINWARING: If I may say, I think you're being very childish,
Frazer. Now, has anybody got any suggestions on how to find
the north?

GODFREY: Moss always grows on the north side of trees, sir
– if that's any help.

Memories ...

'This is one of my favourite episodes. The shot in the studio
was a primitive form of back-projection, with the boat quite still
and the waves very heavy. We had to put up with a lot of tech-
nical difficulties for the simple reason that the solution to
these problems hadn't been found.'

JIMMY PERRY

MAINWARING: It isn't, Godfrey.

JONES: Permission to speak, sir? If you point the hour hand of your watch at the sun, and then halve the angle between that and 12 o'clock, that points to the south.

MAINWARING: It happens to be night, Jones.

WILSON: Perhaps it might help if we pointed it at the moon, sir?

JONES: No, it's got to be the sun, Sergeant – we used to find our way like that in the Sudan. Mind you, we used to get a lot of sun in the Sudan, 'cept at night, of course, we didn't get it at night.

'I was wondering who'd be first to notice that ...' (Mainwaring)

WILSON: If we could find the North Star, that might help, sir.

JONES: You've got to find the Great Bear first – that's the group of stars that looks like a milk saucepan. Now, the stars opposite the handle point to the North Star. In other words, if it was a saucepan, it's where you'd pour the milk.

WALKER: Hence the Milky Way.

'SERGEANT – SAVE MY BOY!'

Pike gets stuck in a minefield on the beach.

JONES: Permission to shout a short message of encouragement to Private Pike, sir?

MAINWARING: Yes, go ahead.

JONES: (*Shouting*) Cheer up, Private Pike, and don't move a muscle or you'll be blown to Kingdom Come.

GODFREY: Poor boy, he must be awfully cold and wet out there.

MRS PIKE: Him with a delicate chest, too. You ought to take more care of him, Mr Mainwaring.

MAINWARING: I'm waging war, Mrs Pike, not running a clinic.

'PUT THAT LIGHT OUT!'

Mainwaring and his men have set up an observation post in the lighthouse. When Jones accidentally turns the light on, illuminating the entire town, Mainwaring tries to sort things out before an air raid. He makes a call from the Jolly Roger Ice Cream Kiosk.

MAINWARING: I'm Captain Mainwaring of the Home Guard.

OPERATOR: Who?

MAINWARING: Captain Mainwaring. MAINWARING.

OPERATOR: Do you want me to write it down?

MAINWARING: No, no. Just listen.

OPERATOR: Yes, I'm listening.

MAINWARING: Now, I'm speaking from the Jolly Roger Ice Cream Parlour.

OPERATOR: That's been shut since the war.

MAINWARING: I know, it is an air raid warden's post and I'm speaking from there at the moment.

OPERATOR: Captain Mainwaring?

MAINWARING: That's right.

OPERATOR: Of the Home Guard?

MAINWARING: Yes.

OPERATOR: Are you an air raid warden as well, then?

MAINWARING: Look, don't worry about that for now. I want you to connect me to the lighthouse.

OPERATOR: I can't, it's cut off.

MAINWARING: I know, I want you to reconnect it.

OPERATOR: Ooh, I can't do that, you'll have to talk to the supervisor.

MAINWARING: That's who I asked for in the first place.

OPERATOR: Here, wait a minute. There's an address here that takes messages for the lighthouse.

MAINWARING: Good, that's the ticket. Give it to me. (*He turns to Wilson*) Pencil, Wilson, take this down.

By accidentally putting Walmington under the spotlight, Jones placed the town in danger.

OPERATOR: It's the Jolly Roger Ice Cream Kiosk.

MAINWARING: The Jolly Roger Ice – look, I'm speaking from there.

OPERATOR: Can't you give the message, then?

WALKER: Here, wait a minute, sir. (*He takes the phone*) Hello, Freda.

OPERATOR: Yes.

WALKER: This is Joe Walker.

OPERATOR: Hello, Joe.

WALKER: Put 71 into 23 will you?

OPERATOR: What you up to, then? Oh, all right, Joe, just a minute.

WALKER: (*Handing back the receiver*) She's putting you through. (*To Wilson*) We used to run the brandy in from France on the motor boats, see – before the war, and this bent coast-guard used to tip me off when they were rounding the bay.

'THE TWO AND A HALF FEATHERS'

Mainwaring and his wife are sleeping in the air-raid shelter. Mainwaring occupies the bottom bunk while the oversized Elizabeth is on top. All we see of her is her outline, about six inches above Mainwaring, who can't sleep.

MAINWARING: Two o'clock. (*He croons softly to the outline above*) Elizabeth – are you awake?

ELIZABETH: Mmmmmmmmmmm.

MAINWARING: You know, dear, I really think it would be better if we slept in the house when there isn't a raid on – this shelter is very damp.

ELIZABETH: Mmmmmmmmmm.

MAINWARING: I just can't sleep – I think I'll read for a while. (*He picks up a small Home Guard manual – props himself upon his elbow and starts to read – Elizabeth turns in her sleep, her outline changes and knocks him back on his pillow*) I think you'd be much more comfortable if I slept in the top bunk, dear.

ELIZABETH: Mmmmmmmmmmm.

Memories ...

'Jones being late in the drill wasn't planned. It came from rehearsals and was funny so we kept it in. An awful lot of things – perhaps as high as 20 per cent – originate from rehearsals; you see something good and keep it in.'

DAVID CROFT

'MUM'S ARMY'

When women are being recruited to join the Walmington Home Guard, Mrs Fox offers her services.

JONES: Mrs Fox is a very fine cooking lady, sir – and most understanding and a warm female person.

MAINWARING: Well, I'm sure that will be most useful. Would you like to join us?

MRS FOX: I didn't know you'd come apart! (*She roars with laughter*)

The jovial Mrs Fox (Pamela Cundell) had a soft spot for Corporal Jones.

Ivy Samways, a friend of Pike's, is also interviewed by Captain Mainwaring.

MAINWARING: You're a shop assistant, aren't you?

She nods.

MAINWARING: Address?

IVY: (*Completely inaudible*) Twenty-seven, Jutland Drive.

MAINWARING: I beg your pardon?

IVY: (*Inaudible again*) Twenty-seven, Jutland Drive.

MAINWARING: I ... I'm afraid I didn't quite catch that.

PIKE: Jutland Drive, sir.

MAINWARING: Oh, Jutland Drive. (*He writes*) What number?

IVY: (*Inaudible*) Twenty-seven.

John Le Mesurier was perfectly cast as Sergeant Wilson.

Memories ...

'Mrs Fox was everybody's favourite character and people still call me Mrs Fox. I based the character on giggly me, really, and had the most wonderful time. She was flamboyant and probably the best character I've played.

'I got the part after appearing in a show with Ian Carmichael. I played a fortune-teller in just one episode. At the end, I had to look at the camera and say: "It will all be revealed at the end." And then I had to wink. David Croft was in the audience and wanted someone to be in Mr Jones' queue at the butcher's and wink after asking whether he had any sausages. And he chose me, because of the wink.

'I also loved the episode, "My British Buddy", partly because I had such flashy clothes to wear. In the episode, there was one line I just couldn't remember. Clive [Dunn] said: "What you want to do is write it on the palm of your hand, then make a gesture and just read it." When it came to the recording, with my nerves my hands had got all sticky and the ink had run. Luckily, I remembered it, anyway.'

PAMELA CUNDELL

MAINWARING: Umh?

IVY: (*Inaudible again*) Twenty-seven.

PIKE: Twenty-seven ... sir.

MAINWARING: Ah ... now I wonder what sort of task we can find to fit Miss Samways?

WILSON: Answering the telephone, sir?

MAINWARING: You're trying my patience rather far today, Wilson.

WILSON: (*Sarcastically*) She can look after the secrets' file, sir, most admirably.

....

Mrs Gray, to whom Mr Mainwaring has taken a fancy, decides to leave Walmington. Mainwaring rushes to the railway station to persuade her to stay.

MAINWARING: What's this then, what's happened?

MRS GRAY: Nothing's happened, I'm just going back to London, that's all.

MAINWARING: How long for?

MRS GRAY: I don't know, a month or two – for good perhaps.

MAINWARING: Why? You never mentioned it – you never even hinted.

MRS GRAY: I just thought it would be best.

MAINWARING: But I don't want you to go. My whole life is completely different. I just live from one meeting to the next.

MRS GRAY: I know, I'm just the same, but it's the only thing to do. People are talking.

MAINWARING: People always talk – who cares about that?

MRS GRAY: But there's your wife.

MAINWARING: They won't talk to her. She's not left home since Munich.

MRS GRAY: Be sensible, George. You can't afford to have scandal and tittle tattle.

MAINWARING: I don't care.

MRS GRAY: But there's the bank.

MAINWARING: Damn the bloody bank!

MRS GRAY: George!

MAINWARING: I'm sorry, but don't take that train.

MRS GRAY: George, I must.

MAINWARING: I implore you – don't take that train; we'll only see each other once a week.

Did you know?

England and Yorkshire cricket legend Freddie Trueman appeared in the 1970 episode, 'The Test', in which the Home Guard play a cricket match against the air raid wardens.

MRS GRAY: You're making this very difficult for me, but I've made up my mind. It's the only way.

The sound of a train approaches in the distance.

PORTER: (*Out of vision*) Victoria – Victoria train.

MRS GRAY: There's my train.

MAINWARING: Fiona, I've never begged anyone for anything in my life, but I'm begging you not to go.

A serviceman comes up with a cup of tea. Mainwaring has risen.

SERVICEMAN: Finished with those chairs, mate?

MAINWARING: Yes, take the damn things.

SERVICEMAN: Oh, all right, I only asked.

MRS GRAY: I'm sorry, George.

She picks up her cases and moves to the door.

MAINWARING: Here, that's heavy. Let me.

Memories ...

'I have fond memories of playing Pikey and wouldn't have missed it for the world. I never think about what roles the character may have stopped me doing because it gave me so many other things to do.

'Some people say Pike was an idiot but I don't agree, he was just naïve. The only time I had a disagreement with David and Jimmy was when they tried making him do things like suck his thumb. I didn't have any problems with him having a teddy bear – I've still got my teddy bear and I'm 61, not that I sleep with him. I said I'd suck my thumb when I've fallen asleep but I'm not going to walk around sucking my thumb, that's stupid. He was definitely a mother's boy and mollycoddled. The fact he wasn't called up was a terrible thing because it would have been the making of him.'

IAN LAVENDER

'"Mum's Army" was slightly based on *Brief Encounter*, but I didn't go as far as using the music, which was a potent factor in the movie. It was a favourite episode of mine. Arthur Lowe didn't like it to begin with. He said: "If I'd read this before we started rehearsal, I'd have had something to say." He was rather against it but within a few days was saying it was "pure genius".'

DAVID CROFT

He helps her with the case. They move on to the platform.

MAINWARING: Look, let's talk about it. Go tomorrow. How do I get in touch with you?

MRS GRAY: You won't be able to.

MAINWARING: You'll write, won't you?

MRS GRAY: Maybe, after a while – I don't know.

PORTER'S VOICE: Stand clear, please.

MAINWARING: But, please, you must … promise me you'll write.

MRS GRAY: Very well – I promise.

The train whistle blows and there is the sound of the train moving off.

'UNINVITED GUESTS'

Mainwaring and his men test out a new form of communication, using tin cans and string!

MAINWARING: (*Speaking into the tin*) Hello, all stations, Charlie One. Hello, all stations, Charlie One. Report my signal, all stations, Charlie One. Over. (*They can't understand a word. He takes his mouth from the tin*) Now, is that quite clear?

FRAZER: Speaking for myself, sir, I didn't understand one single word.

WILSON: I heard you through the tin, it was rather good.

MAINWARING: What I said was, 'Hello, all stations, Charlie One. Hello, all stations, Charlie One. Report my signal, all stations, Charlie One. Over.'

WALKER: What's Charlie One?

MAINWARING: Wilson is Charlie One, but I used his call sign.

WALKER: How do we know who's who?

MAINWARING: Well, it's quite simple, really. I'm saying hello to all of you. You Wilson, are Charlie One. You Frazer, are Charlie Two and Walker is Charlie Three, and so on.

FRAZER: If you're trying to talk to me, why don't you say 'Hello, Charlie Two'?

MAINWARING: Because that's what you say when you talk to me. You say 'Hello, Charlie Two'.

FRAZER: You mean, I say hello to me.

MAINWARING: No, you say hello to me.

FRAZER: Then why don't I say, 'Hello, Charlie One'?

MAINWARING: (*Confused*) Because they don't do it like that.

PIKE: Are we all Charlie Ones, too?

Memories ...

'We never saw Mrs Mainwaring, she was much more potent, as a character, at the end of a telephone. You heard her approaching occasionally or saw her bulge in the top bunk. Just when you think there's a possibility of seeing her, something happens – it's good comedy.'

DAVID CROFT

MAINWARING: For the time being, we will imagine that everyone in this line is headquarters, so we'll say, 'Hello, Charlie One'.

GODFREY: Captain Mainwaring, my name really is Charlie. Does that make any difference?

....

Mainwaring is forced to share the Vicar's office with Hodges. He receives a phone call from his wife.

MAINWARING: There – what did I tell you? (*He takes the receiver*) Good evening, sir – Mainwaring here. Oh – oh, hello, Elizabeth.

WARDEN: You can pack that in. We've no time for your carry-ing on chats with your bits of stuff.

MAINWARING: Will you be quiet, this happens to be my good lady.

WARDEN: Well, cut it short.

MAINWARING: Yes, dear. No, I can't possibly come home now. If you're frightened, dear, can't you go and sit in the cupboard under the stairs as usual? Yes, well I would have thought a bomb was more dangerous than a mouse.

'FALLEN IDOL'

Mainwaring and his men are attending a weekend course at the School of Explosives. Walker, Frazer, Godfrey and three others come in with their bedding.

GODFREY: (*To Walker*) Oh dear, have we got to sleep on the ground?

WALKER: It's either that or stand up all night.

GODFREY: It's not going to do my rheumatics any good.

FRAZER: Ach! Don't be so namby-pamby – it will make your spine go straight.

GODFREY: At my age it's already decided which way it wants to go.

FRAZER: (*Muttering*) Silly old fool.

PIKE: (*Whispering to Wilson*) Uncle Arthur!

WILSON: What is it, Frank?

PIKE: Have you seen Mr Snuggly?

WILSON: Mr who?

PIKE: Mr Snuggly, my teddy.

WILSON: No, I haven't.

PIKE: Mum told me she'd put him in.

WILSON: Well, I haven't seen him.

PIKE: I must find him – I can't get to sleep without him, you know that.

WILSON: I haven't got him.

Sergeant Wilson takes a moment to relax.

PIKE: Have a look – see if he's in your bed.

WILSON: All right. (*He feels down in his bedding and pulls out a teddy bear*) Here he is.

PIKE: Put him back – don't let anybody see him.

WILSON: I thought you wanted him.

PIKE: I don't want anybody to see him, they might laugh at me; wrap him in a towel and pass him over.

'Now, see here, Wilson. I don't want any of this public school rubbish.' (Mainwaring)

Wilson wraps the bear in a towel – Mainwaring sees him.

MAINWARING: What have you got there, Wilson?

WILSON: Mr Snuggly.

MAINWARING: What?

Memories ...

'I don't agree that John Le Mesurier was vague; what he did was he played at being vague to get what he wanted. I saw him persuade a young make-up artist to take the watch off his wrist, wind it up for him and then put it back on. He was getting something done that he couldn't be bothered to do himself!

'I got on with all the cast. John Laurie and I hit it off from the word "Go". He taught me how to do *The Times*' crossword. Like me, he didn't have a lot to do in the first few episodes so had time to talk to a young, green actor about his career.

'I was also very fond of Arthur Lowe. We were all like our characters and he was like Mainwaring – a pompous little man. What you didn't know, until he let you in on it, was that he knew he was a pompous little man. And quite often he'd burst his own bubble. Yes, he was pompous but a lot of the time he was playing along with it.'

IAN LAVENDER

'Arthur was one of the best actors when it came to playing drunks. He actually put in the line, "Damn revolving doors." It was the first time he put a line in.'

JIMMY PERRY

WILSON: (*Unwrapping the bear*) My teddy, sir – I just can't get to sleep without him.

MAINWARING: Extraordinary. (*He turns back to his bedding*)

PIKE: Thanks, Uncle Arthur.

....

Everyone in the platoon is asleep when Mainwaring stumbles into the tent. He's inebriated after sharing a few drinks at the officers' mess.

MAINWARING: (*As he enters the tent, he wobbles and grabs a tent pole to stop himself falling over*) Damn revolving doors!

JONES: Yeow! (*He grabs Mainwaring by the throat while still half asleep, then realises what he's done*) I'm sorry, Mr Mainwaring.

Mainwaring had too many to drink while on exercise.

CHRISTMAS SPECIAL: 'BATTLE OF THE GIANTS'

Jones gets a bout of malaria but Godfrey, the platoon medic, isn't much use.

MAINWARING: Where have you been, Godfrey?

GODFREY: I'm sorry, sir – as we stopped I took the opportunity to be excused.

MAINWARING: Well you'd no right to, as the medic it's your duty to be on hand at all times.

GODFREY: Oh dear – what's wrong with Mr Jones?

MAINWARING: He's got a bout of malaria – have you got anything we can give him?

GODFREY: (*Opening his satchel*) I don't know really, sir.

He takes out some bandages and a bottle of aspirins.

GODFREY: I've got some aspirins, some bicarbonate of soda and some ointment for wasp stings.

MAINWARING: Wasp stings! This is a fighting unit, not a girl guides' outing. What would you do if one of us was wounded?

Mr Mainwaring's meeting with Mrs Fox caused a few raised eyebrows.

Memories ...

'Towards the end of the series, we discovered that Arthur Lowe suffered from narcolepsy, a condition which meant he could drop off at any moment. It got quite serious and I remember him being counted in at the start of a recording and having to say: "Wake him up for god's sake." Someone would go along, shake him and he'd be fine.'

DAVID CROFT

'KEEP YOUNG AND BEAUTIFUL'

When there is talk that older members of the Home Guard may have to join the ARP Wardens, Wilson and Mainwaring take steps to look younger in order to stay in the platoon.

MAINWARING: Wilson, you're wearing corsets!

Wilson doesn't reply.

Did you know?

Dad's Army spin-offs included a long-running stage show and a big screen adaptation, released in 1971. Another film, *Dad's Army and the Secret U-boat Base*, was planned with Sir Laurence Olivier playing a villain. Sadly, it never materialised.

MAINWARING: Well, am I right?

WILSON: Actually, it's a gentleman's abdominal support.

MAINWARING: Gentleman's abdominal support my foot, you're wearing corsets! You're a rum cove, Wilson. You wear that uniform like a sack of porridge, and yet in other respects you're as vain as a peacock.

WILSON: It is nothing whatever to do with vanity. I don't want to risk being put into Hodges' mob, that's all. I'm really quite proud of our platoon. I think you've done a marvellous job putting us all together. I really mean that. So, I think it pays, at the moment, not to look any older than one needs.

'I think you're going in to the realms of fantasy now, Jones.' (Mainwaring)

MAINWARING: I'm sorry, Wilson – it was very kind of you to pay that little tribute. I know that sort of thing isn't easy for a person like you. I was pouring scorn upon you and I have no right to do such a thing. No right at all. I have to tell you that I, too, have taken steps to appear more, well – more virile.

WILSON: My God, not monkey glands?

MAINWARING: Certainly not – nothing as drastic as that. What do you think of this?

He removes his hat, revealing a toupee. Wilson corpses but quickly recovers himself.

WILSON: It's really awfully … (*He giggles again*) It's really awfully good.

Wilson subsides into uncontrollable laughter. Mainwaring is furious.

MAINWARING: Watch out, Wilson, you'll snap your girdle.

'A SOLDIER'S FAREWELL'

Mainwaring has planned a cheese supper with his wife but she's not interested and he can't reach her on the phone. He decides to share it with Wilson instead.

WILSON: Can't you get any answer from her, sir?

MAINWARING: No – it's most strange. Where on earth can she be? (*Looking at cheese*) Doesn't that cheese look delicious, Wilson? (*He breaks off a small piece and eats it*) Hmm! Melts in your mouth.

WILSON: (*Licks his lips*) Does it really?

MAINWARING: Elizabeth will be delighted when I take this home to her tonight. What is she doing? Oh – hello, Elizabeth – you have been a long time answering, dear … Where have you been? Oh, I see … (*To Wilson*) In the air raid shelter. I thought we might sleep in the house tonight, dear – after all we haven't had any raids for a week … Oh. Yes, dear – yes, dear. Anyhow, I might have a little surprise for you tonight: I've bought – what – yes, dear – oh – but, Elizabeth, I … very well. (*He hangs up*)

WILSON: What's the matter, sir?

MAINWARING: She's had her supper and she's going to bed.

> ### Did you know?
> Among the programme's many fans was the Queen Mother, whose favourite episode was 'The Royal Train'.

WILSON: Why didn't you tell her about the cheese?

MAINWARING: She wouldn't listen. You know it's a funny thing about women, Wilson – every time you plan a surprise, somehow it always goes wrong. I was so looking forward to that toasted cheese supper, too. I'll never understand women if I live to be a hundred.

WILSON: Look, sir, why don't we have the toasted cheese supper here?

MAINWARING: What, just the two of us together?

WILSON: Why not, sir? We've got some bread – and I've got these two bottles of milk stout.

MAINWARING: That's very thoughtful of you, Wilson.

WILSON: Thank you, sir.

MAINWARING: You know, someone once wrote somewhere – I forget who it was – 'The love for a woman waxes and wanes like the moon and stars – but the friendship of a man lasts for eternity.' I value your comradeship, Wilson.

WILSON: Thank you, sir.

MAINWARING: By the way, don't forget to pay me for your half of the cheese.

'GETTING THE BIRD'

Walker pops into Jones' shop and offers him a rabbit.

WALKER: How about a nice bit of rabbit, Jonesey?

JONES: You'll be lucky, I haven't seen a rabbit for six weeks.

WALKER: You 'ave now. (*He whips out the dead rabbit from under his coat and slaps it on the counter*)

JONES: Where d'you get that?

WALKER: It's Bugs Bunny – he decided to give up the pictures and help the war effort. It's five bob and I want the skin back.

JONES: What for?

FRAZER: I wouldn't put it past him to get it refilled.

Walker was always looking for an opportunity to make some money.

WALKER: I've got a friend who makes mink coats. Well. You can't get the mink, can you?

....

Over the last few days, Wilson hasn't been himself. The reason is finally revealed in the shape of a daughter no one knew he had. Outside the church, where the platoon is attending a service, Wilson waits for someone. A pretty Wren arrives with a suitcase. Frazer is in the background.

WILSON: Oh dear, you have that case to carry. I am so sorry I couldn't see you off.

GIRL: That's all right. I was afraid I was going to miss you.

WILSON: I'm glad I saw you in uniform – it suits you terribly well.

GIRL: So does yours – I must rush or I'll be late. (*She kisses him*) Goodbye, Daddy.

WILSON: Goodbye, my darling – thank you for coming to see me.

GIRL: I'm very glad I did – goodbye.

She goes – he calls after her.

WILSON: Give my love to your mother.

He turns and sees Frazer – they look at each other – Wilson realises that Frazer has overheard.

FRAZER: She's a fine lassie.

Memories ...

'I've known Clive for years but Jack Haig was first choice to play Jones. Clive had played that kind of part frequently and I didn't want him for that reason. But Jack was offered 26 episodes of a children's programme called *Wacky Jacky*. He met Tom Sloan and asked which part he should take. Tom said he didn't think *Dad's Army* would run to more than 13 and he should take *Wacky* ...

'Someone else who read for the part was David Jason, and did it superbly. I didn't use him because I couldn't face the problem of making him look old; he was about 26 at the time, and the thought of making him up every day would have been a nuisance. So the part was eventually offered to Clive Dunn and wonderful he was, too.'

DAVID CROFT

WILSON: Her mother left me when she was a baby – I've seen very little of her, really, though I did manage to send her to a good school.

FRAZER: She does you credit.

WILSON: Yes, it was worth it, I think. Still, it's all in the past. I didn't really want anyone to know.

FRAZER: I'm an old blabbermouth, but I really promise you that nobody'll ever learn anything of this from me.

WILSON: Thank you, Frazer – that's very kind of you.

Wilson's daughter arrived on the scene in 'Getting the Bird'.

'THE DESPERATE DRIVE OF CORPORAL JONES'

Godfrey's idea of haversack rations isn't quite the same as Mainwaring's, when the platoon prepare for a weekend exercise.

MAINWARING: On the command, 'Fall out', you'll put your kit in Jones' van. (*He sees that Godfrey is carrying a rather large basket*) Godfrey, I don't think we need quite as much first aid kit as that.

GODFREY: It's not first aid, sir, it's my picnic.

MAINWARING: Picnic?

GODFREY: Well you said we were to bring food.

MAINWARING: I said haversack rations – which means sandwiches.

GODFREY: I find that sort of thing awfully indigestible, and my sister has packed me a vegetable flan and some rice pudding.

MAINWARING: Rice pudding! This is war, Godfrey. This is no place for rice pudding. Leave it in my office.

WALKER: With the spoon.

MAINWARING: That's enough, Walker. Right, fall out, the rest of you.

'ALL IS SAFELY GATHERED IN'

The Warden has a narrow escape and thinks it's divine intervention.

WARDEN: Oh, Vicar, thank the Lord I've found you. I must talk to you.

VICAR: Hello, Mr Hodges – I heard you had a narrow escape last night.

WARDEN: Narrow escape – it was a miracle. It landed right there beside me. If it had gone off, I wouldn't be here talking to you now.

VICAR: A miracle indeed.

WARDEN: It knocked my pint right clean out of my hand – look. (*He shows the mug handle in his hand*) It was a deliverance.

Memories ...

'In this episode I had to ride a bike. I was over 30 years younger but, even so, hadn't ridden a bicycle for years. To be confronted by this old boneshaker and asked to ride across an uneven field was quite a challenge. Like so many episodes of *Dad's Army*, it paints an idyllic picture of a Britain that has past, a tranquil countryside – it's wonderfully nostalgic.

'My first episode, though, was "The Armoured Might of Corporal Jones". I only had a couple of lines. The Vicar came across as a very innocent character because the platoon is stealing gas from his vicarage; later on, he became rather fussy. David and Jimmy always wrote lines which gave you an insight into your character, such as his constant irritation with Mr Yeatman; I then suddenly discovered from some of the lines they'd written for Teddy that I was a martyr for whisky! The Vicar was a lovely character to play and I enjoyed it very much.'

FRANK WILLIAMS

VERGER: More like a judgement.

VICAR: Go away, Mr Yeatman.

VERGER: Yes, sir. (*He goes*)

WARDEN: I should have been killed, I was spared – why me? Answer me that – why me – why me – why, why?

VICAR: I can't think.

WARDEN: I'm just a simple greengrocer. Do you think he's saving me for some great purpose?

VICAR: Well, you never know.

WARDEN: All my life I've been rotten, but I'm going to turn over a new leaf. I'm going to be kind to everyone and I'm going to love my enemies, not Hitler, of course, but I'm going to be good to Mainwaring and I'm going to help him with his struggle, because he's a good man at heart, you know.

VICAR: I'm sure he is.

WARDEN: From now on, I'm going to be right behind him.

VICAR: Well, that's marvellous news.

The Vicar (Frank Williams) was a rather huffy individual.

'WHEN DID YOU LAST SEE YOUR MONEY?'

Mainwaring wants to examine Mr Bluett's chicken to check for Jones' missing money. The platoon visits Bluett's home, late at night.

BLUETT: Who is it?

MAINWARING: It's me, Captain Mainwaring.

BLUETT: What's the matter? Have the Germans landed?

MAINWARING: No, I have to speak to you very urgently. Open the door.

Mr Bluett slips the chain and opens the door.

MAINWARING: I understand you had a chicken delivered to you yesterday.

BLUETT: Yes, that's right.

MAINWARING: Have you eaten it yet?

BLUETT: No, and you can't have it back if that's what you want.

'Don't they know there's a war on?' (Mainwaring)

WILSON: Actually, we want to examine it.

BLUETT: Have you got a search warrant?

Did you know?

Arnold Ridley, who played Private Godfrey, was the oldest member of the cast – 72 when it began in 1968. He'd fought in the Great War and was seriously wounded on the Somme, leaving his left arm virtually useless and causing blackouts for the rest of his life. Later on, he became a successful playwright, penning *The Ghost Train* in the 1920s.

'BRAIN VERSUS BRAWN'

Mainwaring is put out when Walker is invited to the Rotary dinner.

WALKER: Evening, Mr Mainwaring.

MAINWARING: What are you doing here, Walker?

WALKER: Why, shouldn't I be here?

MAINWARING: I didn't know that under-the-counter dealing was a profession.

WALKER: 'Tis now. Anyway, if it wasn't for me, you wouldn't be supping that sherry, and the chicken croquettes you're going to have would be made of whale meat instead of rabbit.

'A BRUSH WITH THE LAW'

A junior warden reports to Hodges at the wardens' post.

HODGES: What have you got?

JUNIOR WARDEN: Not bad. Nine forty-five, Miss Samways at the bungalow was showing a light from her bathroom window.

HODGES: Very naughty.

JUNIOR WARDEN: She was using more than five inches of water an' all.

HODGES: Was she?

JUNIOR WARDEN: Right up to here it was. (*He indicates above the chest*)

Memories ...

'I used Bill Pertwee a lot in my shows. He's a very strong actor and could push people around very well. He was a great enthusiast, too, and was good to have in the company – he cheered everybody up. He was the one who went round and said: "Isn't it going marvellously?"'

DAVID CROFT

HODGES: Yes, well, I'll check that myself before we prosecute.
What else?

Hodges (Bill Pertwee) was a constant thorn in Mainwaring's side.

'ROUND AND ROUND WENT THE GREAT BIG WHEEL'

Jones is forever volunteering and shows his bravery.

JONES: I should like to volunteer to be tortured, sir, let me be a guinea pig, let me see how much pain I can stand, let me suffer, sir, I demand to suffer.

FRAZER: Shut up, you silly old fool.

Memories ...

'The most difficult day's filming ever was for this episode. The plot focused on the War Office's new weapon: an explosive-carrying wheel controlled by radio. Operation Catherine Wheel took place to test the new invention, with Mainwaring's men responsible for fatigues.

'We decided that the best way to get the wheel moving was to build a big hub in it and have someone inside peddling. But it didn't work because the whole mechanism collapsed. From then on we kept pushing and filming it as it gradually slowed down. We could only film about 20 feet of movement at any one time – it took ages!'

DAVID CROFT

'TIME ON MY HANDS'

Mainwaring believes in fair dealing but it doesn't extend to the biscuits when he visits the Marigold Tea Rooms with Wilson.

Miss Fortescue appears with the coffee.

MISS FORTESCUE: Two coffees and three rich tea biscuits.

WILSON: Thank you, very much.

MISS FORTESCUE: Thank you. (*She goes*)

Wilson and Mainwaring each take a biscuit.

MAINWARING: I don't approve of black market activities, as you know. I believe in fair share for all. (*He takes the last biscuit and puts it on his plate*)

WILSON: So do I.

*Wilson takes the biscuit off Mainwaring's plate – breaks it –
takes half himself and puts half back on Mainwaring's plate.
Mainwaring reacts.*

Mainwaring and Wilson regularly frequented the Marigold Tea Rooms.

'THE DEADLY ATTACHMENT'

When a U-boat captain and his crew are fished out of the sea, Mainwaring's platoon is tasked with guarding them temporarily. It's not long before the insults begin flying.

MAINWARING: I shall have a word with the prisoners, Wilson.

WILSON: But you don't speak German.

MAINWARING: Oh, they'll know by the tone of my voice who's in charge, believe me, Wilson, they recognise authority. (*To the prisoners*) Right now, pay attention.

WILSON: They're awfully well disciplined, sir.

MAINWARING: Nothing of the sort, it's a slavish, blind obedience, not like the cheerful, light-hearted discipline that you get with our Jolly Jack Tars. I tell you, they're a nation of unthinking automatons, led by a lunatic who looks like Charlie Chaplin.

The German U-boat captain prepares to jot down some names.

U-BOAT CAPTAIN: How dare you compare our glorious leader with that non-Aryan clown? (*He takes out a notebook*) I am making a note of your insults, captain. Your name will go on the list, and when we win the war, you will be brought to account.

MAINWARING: You can put down what you like, you're not going to win the war.

CAPTAIN: Oh yes we are.

MAINWARING: Oh no you're not.

PIKE: (*Sings*) Whistle while you work, Hitler is a twerp, he's half barmy, so's his army, whistle …

CAPTAIN: Your name will also go on the list. What is it?

MAINWARING: Don't tell him, Pike!

CAPTAIN: Pike, thank you.

Memories ...

'John Le Mesurier and Arthur Lowe seemed to be like their characters. We were in the pub one evening and Arthur was sitting on a stool at the bar. The door opened and someone walked in. He wasn't anything to do with us and from the look on Arthur's face, you'd think he was intruding. It was as if the man didn't have any right to be in the pub!

'Although I know the episode well, of course, the jokes still make me laugh. To laugh after all these years shows the quality of the writing. I've done plenty of work but am still remembered for playing the U-boat captain. People shout across the street, "Don't tell 'em, Pike!" The fact Mainwaring said it seems irrelevant.

'And I was holidaying in the Mongolian Desert, the other year. We were on a camel trek and this guy asked: "Are you the man who played the U-boat captain in *Dad's Army*?" I couldn't believe it.'

PHILIP MADOC

'THE ROYAL TRAIN'

Mainwaring has been to the chemist for Mrs Mainwaring.

MAINWARING: I had to pop into the chemist for Mrs Mainwaring – and, of course, they made me wait.

WILSON: Oh dear, nothing serious I hope.

'I would like to volunteer, sir!' (Jones)

MAINWARING: No, not really. She doesn't sleep that's all. It's the raids.

WILSON: We haven't had any lately.

MAINWARING: No, but she imagines them just the same. She's a very highly strung woman, you know.

Memories ...

'Filming on the railway track seemed rather hazardous. In the plot, Pikey is driving the train. But Ian, with all his talent, is not a train driver so a proper driver was out of sight and couldn't see what was happening. When the train was chasing us, Bill Pertwee said: "They can't see us and it's going to crash into us. I think we'll have to jump for it soon." I said we'd break our legs if we did, but he shouted: "Better that than have the train crash into us." It all turned out well in the end, and we were perfectly safe, but it seemed dangerous at the time.'

FRANK WILLIAMS

WILSON: So you've said.

MAINWARING: The slightest noise and she'll toss and turn until sunrise. The lid blew off the dustbin last night and before you could say Jack Robinson she was under my bunk with her gas mask on. It took me twenty minutes to persuade her to come out. Then, of course, she had fluff all over her nightgown and I started to brush it off and – ooh, there was a terrible set to.

> ## Did you know?
> Captain Mainwaring's wife, Elizabeth, is never seen. But Arthur Lowe's wife, actress Joan Cooper, played Godfrey's sister, Dolly, and two other characters in the series.

'WE KNOW OUR ONIONS'

The platoon takes part in efficiency tests but Godfrey has trouble keeping up.

CAPTAIN RAMSEY: Now, I want you to be alert and on your toes at all times. What do I want?

ALL: Alert and on our toes at all times.

RAMSEY: Stand up.

They stand.

RAMSEY: Sit down, too slow. Stand up, sit down.

RAMSEY: Up, down, up, down.

GODFREY: Excuse me, sir, I think I missed one. Shall I stand up and sit down again?

Arthur Lowe relaxes with his wife and actress, Joan Cooper.

Memories ...

'Arthur Lowe was a very good comedy actor – extremely clever. He had wonderful technique: nowadays, many actors can't do double-takes and things like that, but as well as being a great comedy actor, he was a great technician and knew his trade.

'As a person he was a little pompous. I got on well with him and we had a huge thing in common: that we'd done years of weekly rep. Regarding not being particularly keen when it came to learning his lines, in fairness to Arthur, he'd done so much weekly rep, always having to cram the words in, sitting up all night studying, this gave him a thing about taking a script home. He'd done it all his life and had reached the point where he didn't like learning lines anymore. Later on, when we could edit, we were able to sharpen his performance by editing out some "umms and arrs" – and he didn't seem to know that we'd done it.

'He was a man of habits. He liked his food and, particularly, Mr Kipling's cakes. He rang me once, just before we were going filming, and said: "I've got the scripts." Instead of talking to me about them, he wanted to ask about the new assistant floor manager. He said: "Have you told the boy about Mr Kipling cakes? I don't want any trouble, see that there is always Mr Kipling cakes for tea. Last season, they had to go a local baker to get the cakes and they weren't a match."'

JIMMY PERRY

'THE HONOURABLE MAN'

Pike wants a go on the platoon's motorbike and says his mum has warned Wilson, who will be riding the bike, not to come home injured.

PIKE: Mum says if he comes home with his face scratched and his arm in a sling, she'll give him what for.

MAINWARING: Look, Pike, who's running the platoon – me or your mother?

PIKE: Well, he's more frightened of Mum.

MAINWARING: Is he indeed.

Mainwaring is put out when Wilson receives a title and becomes a member of the golf club.

WILSON: There's no reason why it should make any difference to us.

MAINWARING: You can bet your bottom dollar it won't make any difference – and you needn't think you can start rolling in twenty minutes late after lunch. Where have you been?

WILSON: I popped up and had a bite at the golf club.

MAINWARING: Who took you to the golf club?

WILSON: I'm a member.

MAINWARING: You're a member? Since when?

WILSON: Well, they heard about this title thing and they asked me if I'd join.

MAINWARING: I've been trying to get in that golf club for years.

WILSON: Yes, I believe they're awfully particular.

'THINGS THAT GO BUMP IN THE NIGHT'

The platoon spends the night in a deserted house and Godfrey is too afraid to go to the bathroom alone.

GODFREY: (*Shaking him*) Mr Frazer!

FRAZER: What's the matter?

GODFREY: I've got to go to the little boy's room, would you mind coming with me, please?

FRAZER: Nothing would make me move from this room. There's too many unnatural causes.

GODFREY: Well, I'm worried about the natural causes.

Mr Frazer (John Laurie) was Walmington's doom-and-gloom merchant.

Memories ...

'Casting John Laurie was Michael Mills' suggestion. He said we should make him a fisherman, which we did in the early episodes but, of course, it was damned useless because fishing boats couldn't go out so he wasn't allowed to go fishing! We had him making coffins in one of the early episodes and before long he'd taken over the funeral business.'

DAVID CROFT

'THE RECRUIT'

Mainwaring is in hospital recovering from an operation on ingrowing toenails. Jones visits with a 'Get Well' present.

MAINWARING: Great Scott – grapes. I haven't seen them since 1939. (*He eats one*)

JONES: Well, they're not real grapes, sir. We impersonated them out of the electric light flex and shaved gooseberries.

MAINWARING: (*Has just bitten a gooseberry and got the sour taste*) I see what you mean.

JONES: The gooseberry fur gave us a bit of bother, and then Mr Frazer found a bit of very, very fine glass paper what he finishes his ten-guinea coffins with and that seemed to answer it.

Mr Jones' present was unpalatable.

....

Mainwaring blames active service for his ingrowing toenails.

WILSON: Are you going to try for a disablement pension?

MAINWARING: Oh no, nothing like that – but mark my words, it's all that standing about that's done it.

Memories ...

'Getting Arthur Lowe to take a script home was difficult. I think this dated from the time he was in repertory, when he almost had a photographic memory; he thought he still had one but didn't. Some people got fed up with him, particularly John Le Mesurier, who'd say: "Can't he learn the bloody thing, rather than doing it in our time?" This accounted for the sudden hesitations you got from Arthur which seemed like wonderful timing but was usually, "What the hell am I going to say next?"

'Focusing on class issues worked very well so we continued to touch on it. It was very relevant to the British way of life, particularly at that time. It was a wonderful stroke when Michael Mills secured the services of John Le Mesurier; Michael saw him playing the officer, but making him the sergeant and chief clerk at the bank, while Arthur Lowe was the captain and bank manager, meant we could exploit the class issues more.'

DAVID CROFT

WILSON: You do an awful lot of sitting about as well – have you had any trouble there?

MAINWARING: You have a very coarse streak, Wilson. You got it at that public school, I suppose.

> ### Did you know?
> *Dad's Army* has its own appreciation society (www.dadsarmy.co.uk) and was voted fourth in a 2004 BBC poll to find Britain's all-time favourite sitcom.

....

The Vicar explains why he joined the Home Guard.

VICAR: It was a spontaneous thing – I'm rather like that, you know. I've been wrestling with my conscience for some time.

VERGER: It's been agony. He was wrestling night and day – I can vouch for that.

Mainwaring and Wilson, colleagues in the bank and comrades in the Home Guard.

Memories ...

'David and I went to public schools and we always exploited the issue of class in our work because it was funny. The whole British nation is obsessed with class and we were both brought up in a class-ridden world. If you went to a public school and wore the tie, you didn't need any qualifications.'

JIMMY PERRY

VICAR: Thank you, Mr Yeatman. Finally, I asked myself: could I stand by and watch my wife being raped by a Nazi? No, I said to myself, I couldn't.

'They don't like it up 'em!' (Jones)

MAINWARING: But you're not married.

VICAR: I have a very vivid imagination.

'A MAN OF ACTION'

Pike tells of his childhood love for bananas.

PIKE: I used to love a big plate of bananas and cream, all mashed up with plenty of sugar. I'd take a big mouthful and press it with my tongue through the gaps in my teeth. Did you like pressing bananas and cream through the gaps in your teeth, Mr Jones?

JONES: No, but I don't mind doing it with blancmange.

PIKE: And jelly?

JONES: Yes, jelly's all right, but not bananas, not at my age with this upper set, it's too risky.

'GORILLA WARFARE'

The platoon plans a weekend exercise and Mainwaring is to be a highly important secret agent.

PIKE: Are you really going to drop out of an aeroplane by parachute, Mr Mainwaring?

MAINWARING: Of course not, you stupid boy, it's a hypothetical parachute.

JONES: I shouldn't use one of them, sir, they're not safe.

Memories ...

'Although the catchphrase, "Stupid boy!" is what my father used to say, most of the other catchphrases happened by accident, such as John Laurie's "I'm Doomed!". He said the line once and we used it again. When I was in the army, we had bayonet drill and the instructor, a drill sergeant, would always say, "They Don't Like it Up em!" As for "Is that wise, sir?", that was a half-hearted catchphrase that John Le Mesurier said and we kept it in. He was always apprehensive about what steps Mainwaring would take in a crisis. We ended up loving the catchphrases and used them at every opportunity, but they have to evolve naturally.'

JIMMY PERRY

'THE GODIVA AFFAIR'

Mrs Fox misunderstands Mainwaring, who's talking to her at the Marigold Tea Rooms on behalf of Jones, and thinks he's become an admirer.

MAINWARING: The point is, Mrs Fox, Jones is a very loyal member of my platoon and I don't want him hurt.

MRS FOX: We won't hurt him, Mr Mainwaring.

'Permission to speak, sir!' (Jones)

MAINWARING: We!

MRS FOX: He can have Mondays and Saturdays, and you can have Tuesdays and Fridays.

Memories ...

'Mr Gordon, the town clerk, was a pompous northerner but wonderful to play. This is my favourite episode. I mention that Mrs Fox will be perfectly respectable, covered from top to toe in fleshings, and wearing a wig of long golden tresses. I mouthed every syllable of those lines while drooling over the thought of Mrs Fox with her ample figure wearing fleshings.'

ERIC LONGWORTH

MAINWARING: Madam, I'm talking about Mr Gordon, the town clerk.

MRS FOX: Well, he can have Wednesdays.

Mrs Fox is auditioning to play Lady Godiva.

MR GORDON: Quiet please, Mrs Fox will be perfectly respectable, covered from top to toe in fleshings, and wearing a wig of long golden tresses.

FRAZER: You'll never cover her with golden tresses, you'll need a bell tent.

Did you know?

Jimmy Beck, who played Private Walker, started out as a commercial artist, and proved himself a talented painter even after his acting career took off.

'THE CAPTAIN'S CAR'

Lady Maltby decides who should be given her Rolls-Royce to help with the war effort.

LADY MALTBY: Now, the thing is, who would make the best use of it, the Home Guard or the Wardens?

MAINWARING: Definitely the Home Guard.

LADY MALTBY: I'm glad you think so. That Mr Hodges seemed awfully common – and I know Mr Jones and, of course, Arthur is such a dear.

Mainwaring reacts.

LADY MALTBY: (*Referring to Mainwaring*) And I'm sure you're very nice when one gets to know you.

'TURKEY DINNER'

Mainwaring tries to cheer up the platoon with a joke.

MAINWARING: Oh, yes. Now, these three Tommies were sitting in the mess hall, and the Scotsman said to the Englishman, 'Pass the semolina pudding', and the Englishman said, 'No, I won't'. Then the Scotsman said, 'Why not?'. To which the Englishman replied, 'Because King's Regulations specifically state: Never help another soldier to desert'.

....

Jones compliments Mrs Fox on her cooking.

JONES: Mrs Fox is the finest cook I ever came across. Haven't I always said you're the finest cook, Mrs Fox?

MRS FOX: Well, you've always been very nice about my dumplings.

'RING DEM BELLS'

The platoon is taking part in a training film and Mainwaring wonders which is his best side.

MAINWARING: Tell me, Wilson, which do you think is my best side?

WILSON: Well, sir, your nose does look a little red from this side. Turn the other way. (*Mainwaring turns*) Yes, it looks a bit red from this side as well. I don't think you've got a best side.

Memories ...

'This was a favourite episode of mine with John Le Mesurier and me dressed as German officers. For the filming, John and I had comfortable costumes to wear because we were playing officers. The uniforms were beautifully tailored rather than the rubbish we were wearing all the time. It was a funny script and David and Jimmy virtually gave me carte blanche to do what I wanted when pretending to be a German officer.'

IAN LAVENDER

Ian Lavender found the German uniform more comfortable than the Home Guard garb.

'WHEN YOU'VE GOT TO GO'

Jones reassures Mainwaring that he can still shoot even though he's hurt his finger.

JONES: Mr Mainwaring, you don't have to worry about it being my trigger finger. I'm amphibious.

> ## Did you know?
> A pilot for a prospective American version, *The Rear Guard*, was shown in 1976 but a full series wasn't commissioned.

Memories ...

'This was another favourite of mine. Pike receives his call-up papers and a fish and chip supper is organised for him. The supper was a wonderful scene, a mixture of slapstick, comedy, sentimentality and pathos.'

IAN LAVENDER

'IS THERE HONEY STILL FOR TEA?'

The bank has suffered bomb damage during an air raid. With his office door ruined, Mainwaring is given a paper door as a temporary replacement, much to his disgust.

MAINWARING: (*To Wilson*) How am I supposed to see important clients in an office with a paper door?

WILSON: Well, they have paper doors in Japan.

MAINWARING: What's that got to do with it?

WILSON: I don't know really.

MAINWARING: And how are people going to knock on it?

WILSON: You could put a notice, 'Don't knock, cough'.

Memories ...

'John Le Mesurier was wonderfully laid back and vague. One day, when we were on the stage tour, he said to me: "Frank, what do you do about your dirty washing when you're on tour?" I replied: "I find a laundry that will do it on the Monday and have it ready for the Saturday." He turned to Teddy [Sinclair] and asked him. Teddy told him he took it down the launderette. He said, astonished: "You mean you sit there and watch it going round and around? I couldn't do that." So I asked what he did, and he said: "Well, I just leave it in my room and somehow some kind person always comes and does it for me." So that's it, how to be helpless and make a feature of it!'

FRANK WILLIAMS

Pikey tries out Mainwaring's new door.

'THE FACE ON THE POSTER'

Mainwaring wants to recruit new people to the platoon and has a poster designed to help. Trouble is, everyone wants to be the face of the campaign. A vote is taken to see whose face will appear on the recruitment poster.

VICAR: (*Reading*) Captain Mainwaring has one.

They all applaud.

WILSON: Congratulations, sir.

MAINWARING: Very gratifying, I must say.

VICAR: Just a minute, Captain Mainwaring. I'm announcing the result in reverse order. Captain Mainwaring has one vote.

WILSON: I thought we'd all agreed not to vote for ourselves.

Memories ...

'John Le Mesurier was like Wilson and played that part all his life. When it came to learning the scripts, he always knew every word and I'm sure he had a photographic memory; he'd say: "Don't tell me, it's on the top of Page 15." He visualised the page.

'Michael [Mills] was a great head of department and, naturally, when he read a script he mentally cast it. I think he made the first contact with John. He said we should have him because he suffers so well. He was perfect for Wilson.'

DAVID CROFT

Memories ...

'I have nothing but fond memories of playing Hodges. I'll always remember the early morning coach trip from the hotel to where we filmed the battle scenes. It was only a few miles and the countryside was beautiful. The weather was always good. We had nothing but sunshine for our filming; in all the years we went there, we only had three days of rain and one of snow.

'It's extraordinary. I've been to places all over the British Isles and people will come up and talk to me about *Dad's Army*. And whenever the programme is chosen as the theme for a charity function, it's always a success. People go mad and won't let us go. They know all the lines, the episodes and often things many of the cast have forgotten. The affection for the programme is unbelievable.'

BILL PERTWEE

'WAKE-UP WALMINGTON'

Mainwaring and his men aim to shake the residents of Walmington out of their complacency by roaming around dressed as Fifth Columnists. Godfrey, meanwhile, is tasked with manning the phone back at the church hall. He awaits a call from Mainwaring but has to spend a penny first, leaving the Verger to answer the phone.

Mainwaring calls.

VERGER: Hello.

MAINWARING: Wake-up, Roger.

VERGER: Eh?

MAINWARING: Wake-up, Roger.

VERGER: My name's not Roger and I haven't been asleep.

MAINWARING: Who's that?

VERGER: It's me, the Verger.

MAINWARING: Where's Godfrey?

VERGER: He's just popped out for a minute. He's asked me to mind the phone.

'Is that wise, sir?' (Wilson)

MAINWARING: Well, he'd no business to. When he comes back, give him this message: 'Operation Wake-Up, Roger', and tell him to ring 633. It's urgent. Got that?

VERGER: Yes, I've got it. (*He writes*) 633.

Mainwaring hangs up. Soon after, Godfrey enters.

VERGER: Captain Mainwaring's just been on the phone for you. He left a message.

GODFREY: What was it?

VERGER: Er … oh yes, let me see, someone named Roger is having an operation … you've got to ring that number right away – it must be the hospital.

GODFREY: (*Picking up phone*) Oh dear, I hope it's not serious. 'Hello, Walmington 633, please.'

Did you know?

Jones' butcher's van now resides at the Patrick Motor Museum in Birmingham. Visits can be booked on 0121 459 4656.

VERGER: It could be appendicitis, it comes on very quick, you know.

GODFREY: Did Captain Mainwaring say anything else?

VERGER: Yes, he said you're not to go to sleep.

GODFREY: I won't do that.

Godfrey rings Mainwaring, who's waiting at a flour mill. Mainwaring picks up the phone.

GODFREY: Hello, is that the hospital?

MAINWARING: What? Is that you, Godfrey?

'Napoleon!' (Hodges)

GODFREY: Yes, sir, how's Roger? Is he going to be all right?

MAINWARING: What are you babbling about?

GODFREY: I got a message that Roger had been taken ill with appendicitis and was having an operation.

MAINWARING: (*Blows hard through frustration*) The message was that Operation Wake-Up had started.

Memories ...

'Arnold Ridley did a good job. Like some of the others, he went into *Dad's Army* when his career was nearly finished and suddenly enjoyed a new lease of life. He was the oldest member of the cast but very good. Strangely, Mr Godfrey is the favourite character of many children. As for the weak bladder, I don't think I'd have included this for the sake of a laugh if I was starting the series now. I don't find old ailments funny now because I'm old myself. Everyone laughs at incontinency but it's no joke. But we didn't make a great thing of it.'

JIMMY PERRY

'THE MAKING OF PRIVATE PIKE'

Jones and Pike discuss a staff car Mainwaring has just received.

PIKE: Did you have staff cars in the Sudan, Mr Jones?

'Ruddy hooligans!' (Hodges)

JONES: No, nothing like that in those days. We had a staff camel once. It was very good in the desert, but it didn't have a horn and windscreen wipers, or anything like that.

'THE MISER'S HOARD'

Frazer is penning a letter to one of his customers.

FRAZER: 'Dear Mrs Pickering. I hope you found the funeral arrangements for your late husband entirely satisfactory. May I say how sorry I was that the hearse ran out of petrol just outside the cemetery. I'm sure your dear departed husband would have been proud of the way you helped to push him to his final resting place. And what a fine strong woman your mother is. I hope you managed to get the mud off her skirt. I enclose my final account.'

'NEVER TOO OLD'

It's the final scene in the closing episode. Jones has just married Mrs Fox but has been called out because there is an invasion alert. It turns out, of course, to be a false alarm. The platoon decides to toast Jones and the Home Guard, but not before Hodges ridicules Mainwaring and his men.

WILSON: So Hitler will not be coming tonight after all.

HODGES: Just as well, with you lot guarding us.

MAINWARING: What do you mean?

HODGES: Well, look at you. What good would you lot be against real soldiers? They'd walk straight through you. Good night.

JONES: Here, he'd no business …

MAINWARING: Take no notice of him, men. (*Mainwaring raises his mess tin*) Here's to your future happiness, Jones.

ALL: Here's to you, Jones.

PIKE: Mr Mainwaring, the Warden wasn't right was he, saying the Nazis would walk right through us?

Individuals in life, but one in adversity.

MAINWARING: Of course he wasn't right.

JONES: I'll tell you one thing: they won't walk straight through me.

FRAZER: Nor me – I'll be beside you, Jonesy.

MAINWARING: We'll all be beside you, Jones. We stand together, make no mistake about that. If anyone tries to take our home or our freedom away from us, they'll find out what we can do. We'll fight and we're not alone. There are thousands of us all over England.

'Put that light out!' (Hodges)

FRAZER: And Scotland.

MAINWARING: And Scotland. All over the British Isles, in fact. Men who will stand together whenever Britain needs them.

WILSON: Do you know, sir, I think it would be rather nice if we paid our own small tribute to them.

MAINWARING: For once, I agree with you, Wilson. 'To Britain's Home Guard'.

They all raise their mugs.

ALL: **To Britain's Home Guard.**

Corporal Jones and Mrs Fox finally tied the knot.

Memories ...

'Towards the end of this episode, there's a scene where Mr Mainwaring and Mrs Fox can't get through the door at the same time. It was originally an accident in rehearsal and Arthur and I laughed; David [Croft] wasn't so pleased, though, and asked us to get it right on the actual take. Arthur turned to me and said: "Don't worry about David, let's do the same thing on the take." So we did and the audience fell about.'

PAMELA CUNDELL

TEST YOUR KNOWLEDGE

Now, fall in, everybody. It's time to find out how much you know about life in and around Walmington-on-Sea. Try our *Dad's Army* quiz …

1. Which episode spotlighted the Americans' arrival in Walmington?

2. Godfrey's sister Dolly is well-known for making what type of cakes?

3. What's the name of the ice cream parlour on Walmington sea front which is mentioned occasionally?

4. What is Mrs Fox's Christian name?

5. What is Private Sponge's occupation?

6. Which well-known actor, who also appeared in *Porridge*, played Dr McCeavedy in 'The Miser's Hoard'?

7. What is the Vicar's name?

8. What does Frazer lose in 'No Spring for Frazer'?

9. What was the name of the female bank clerk who appeared in Series One but was never seen again?

10. The Verger's wife appeared in several episodes – which actress brought her to life?

Answers

1) My British Buddy; 2) Upside-Down Cakes; 3) Jolly Roger Ice Cream Parlour; 4) Marcia; 5) Sheep farmer; 6) Fulton Mackay; 7) Timothy Farthing; 8) The butterfly spring from the Lewis gun; 9) Janet King; 10) Olive Mercer